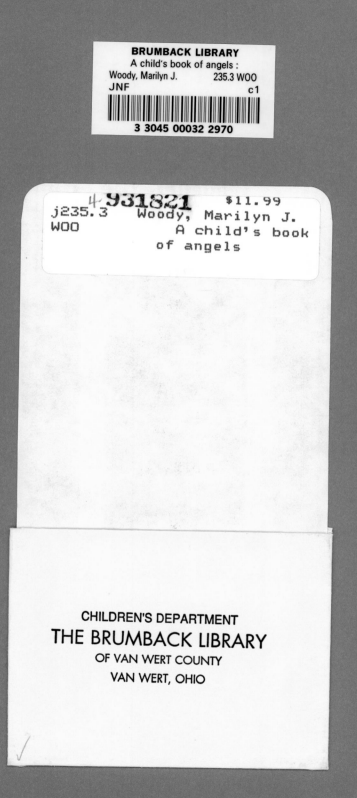

A CHILD'S BOOK OF ANGELS

Stories from the Bible
About God's Special Messengers

Marilyn J. Woody

Chariot Books™
David C. Cook Publishing Co.

Dedicated to my precious
grandchildren—
Jennifer, Katie, Alisha,
and Jeremiah.
May God's mighty
angel helpers
comfort and encourage.

VK DB BM

Chariot Books™ is an imprint of David C. Cook Publishing Co.
David C. Cook Publishing Co., Elgin, Illinois 60120
David C. Cook Publishing Co., Weston, Ontario
Nova Distribution Ltd., Newton Abbot, England

A CHILD'S BOOK OF ANGELS
©1992 by Marilyn J. Woody for text.
©1992 by Illustrators for illustrations bearing their name: by Ami Blackshear, Jesse Reisch, Terry Julien, Rocky Gough,
Kristi Schaeppi, Tim Jonke, Scott Holladay, Krystyna Stasiak, David Slonim, and Jeanne Arnold.
©1992 by David C. Cook Publishing Co. for illustrations bearing illustrator's name: Fred Schnaple, Ron DiCianni, and
Richard Williams.

Designed by Terry Julien
Cover illustration by Kristi Schaeppi

Scriptures are taken from the *Holy Bible: New International Version.* © 1973, 1978, 1984 by the
International Bible Society. Used by permission of Zondervan Bible Publishers.
First Printing, 1992
Printed in Singapore
96 95 94 93 92 5 4 3 2 1
Library of Congress Cataloging-in-Publication Data
Woody, Marilyn J.
A child's book of angels/by Marilyn J. Woody.
p. cm.
Summary: Retells fourteen stories about angelic appearances in th bible, including angels who rejoiced over
the creation of the world: appeared to Paul, Abraham, Elijah, and Mary; and celebrated Jesus' birth.
ISBN 1-55513-756-3
1. Angels--Juvenile literature. 2. Bible stories, English.
[1. Angels. 2. Bible stories.] I. Title
BT962.w66 1992
235'.3--dc20
92-12862
CIP
AC

■   ■   ■

*A*s children read and hear these biblical accounts about God's helpers, they may ask, "What do angels *really* look like?" Illustrators through the ages have drawn their ideas, but the Bible gives only a few details. The important thing is the comforting reality of their existence and ability to minister to all who love God. Come along with me and learn about these majestic beings of God's creation.

Marilyn J. Woody

"Then the glory of the Lord rose from above the cherubim and moved to the threshold of the temple. The cloud filled the temple, and the court was full of the radiance of the glory of the Lord." Ezekiel 10:4

*Dear God,
I want to praise You, too,
like the seraphim
and cherubim.
The whole world is full
of Your glory!*

Have you ever felt the warm sun on your face or the wind blowing your hair? Have you heard the birds singing and seen the brightly colored flowers? These are all ways that God's beautiful world gives Him praise.

In heaven, special angels called cherubim and seraphim are always worshiping and praising God. The seraphim sing, "Holy, holy, holy is the Lord Almighty; the whole earth is full of his glory."

God loves to hear *you* sing and pray, too. It makes Him happy when you think about Him. When you first wake up, when you go to bed, or anytime during the day, you can just tell Him, "I sure do love You, God."

(Isaiah 6:1-6; Ezekiel 10)

Illustration by Ami Blackshear

■　　　■　　　■

"Last night an angel of the God whose I am and whom I serve stood beside me and said, 'Do not be afraid, Paul.' "
Acts 27:23, 24

*D*o you ever feel afraid? Sometimes even big, strong men get scared. That's what happened in this story.

A follower of Jesus named Paul was on a ship with many other men. As they sailed along, wild winds began to blow, and the ship creaked and groaned. The sky turned black, and the men couldn't see the sun or stars. For fourteen days, they had no food to eat.

They were so frightened. *Perhaps we will die,* they thought.

Then an angel came to Paul in the night and said, "Do not be afraid. You and everyone else on the ship will live."

Imagine how surprised and happy Paul was to hear that angel's good news!

We know that God is always watching over us. When we're in danger and afraid, He may even send His angel helpers to protect us.

(Acts 27:13-44)

Dear God, Sometimes I get really scared. Help me to trust You when I'm afraid.

6

Illustration by Jesse Reisch

"Do not forget to entertain strangers, for by so doing some people have entertained angels without knowing it."
Hebrews 13:2

*S*ometimes God uses His angels as mail carriers to deliver special messages. In this story, the angels looked just like ordinary people.

One day a man named Abraham saw three men coming toward his tent-home. They had been traveling and were tired and hungry. Abraham and his wife, Sarah, fixed them a picnic to eat under the trees.

Then one of the men said to Abraham, "Next year Sarah will have a son."

Abraham was amazed at this news. He was almost a hundred years old, and Sarah was ninety. Why, they were old enough to be grandparents, not a new mom and dad!

"Is anything too hard for the Lord?" one of the men asked Abraham.

Later, Abraham found out that the men were really angels. God had sent them to bring the happy announcement about the baby.

Dear God,
Help me to be kind
and loving to people
I meet.

Perhaps you have seen an angel, too, and never even knew it! When you and your family are kind to homeless, sick, or hungry people, you may be helping an angel. You never know!

(Genesis 18:1-15)

8

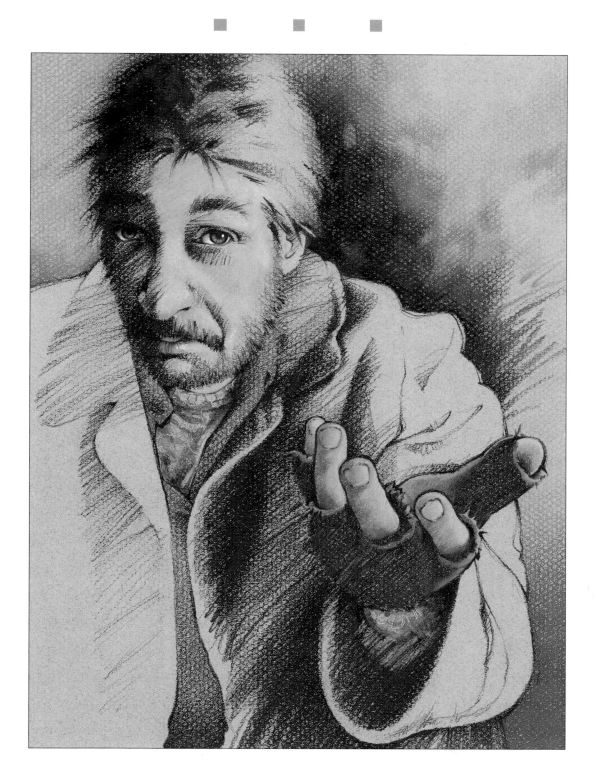

Illustration by Terry Julien

■　　　■　　　■

Elijah was a prophet—a man sent by God to tell people how to live. He loved God with all his heart. When he saw people kneeling and praying to statues of wood or stone, he got very angry. He told them, "It is wrong to bow down to idols. You should pray only to God."

A bad queen named Jezebel told Elijah she would kill him for telling people about the one true God. Elijah ran from Jezebel until he was so tired he fell asleep under a tree.

Then an angel came and touched Elijah. "Get up!" the angel said.

Elijah was surprised. He found hot baked bread and a jar of cool water. After he ate, he had so much energy he didn't get hungry again for forty days!

God knows when you feel worried and lonely, too. Isn't it comforting to think about all the ways He helps us? When His servant Elijah was in need, God even sent an angel.

(I Kings 19:1-8)

*Dear God,
The Bible says You have thousands of angels. I'm glad such a great God never leaves me alone.*

Illustration by Rocky Gough

■   ■   ■

"The morning stars sang together and all the angels shouted for joy." Job 38:7

Have you ever wondered how the sun knows when to go down, or who hangs the stars in the sky? Where is the wind stored? How does the rain know when to fall?

God is the One in charge of the world. After all, He made it.

"Hurray! Hurray! God is making a new world!" God's angels shouted for joy as they watched Him form the sky, the oceans, the flowers, the sun, and the mountains. They saw the birds, the fish, the puppies, and the kittens spring to life. No wonder the angels were so excited!

Dear God, You sure had great ideas when You created the world. Thank You for making me to enjoy it, just as the angels do!

And just think . . . every day you get to see the beautiful world that the angels watched God make. Clouds, rain, snow, and even wild animals. Didn't God have wonderful ideas? And best of all, He made you and me!

(Job 38, 39)

12

Illustration by Kristi Schaeppi

■　　　■　　　■

"Peter was sleeping between two soldiers, bound with two chains, and sentries stood guard at the entrance. Suddenly an angel of the Lord appeared and a light shone in the cell."
Acts 12:6, 7

Peter was arrested and put in prison because he loved Jesus and told other people about Him. He was guarded there by two soldiers. While Peter sat in his prison cell, his friends prayed that he would be set free soon. Can you guess what happened?

The night before Peter was to go before the king who had put him in prison, an angel suddenly appeared to him. A bright light filled Peter's cell, and he felt a tap on his side.

"Quick, get up!" said the angel. The chains fell off Peter's wrists. "Put your clothes on, Peter, and follow me."

Peter never got dressed so fast in all his life!

The angel opened the prison gates, and he and Peter walked right past the sleeping guards!

Even when things look very bad, God knows what's happening. He hears when you pray, and He may use His angels to help answer your prayers.

Dear God,
Help me to be faithful to
You as Peter was.
Thank You for hearing
me when I pray.

(Acts 12:1-19)

Illustration by Fred Schnaple

"My God sent His angel, and he shut the mouths of the lions. They have not hurt me." Daniel 6:22

Have you ever gone to the zoo? The powerful lions are fun to see, but not to touch! They are kept in big caves with fences around them so they cannot hurt you.

But once a man named Daniel got very close to some hungry lions.

Daniel loved God with all his heart. The king wanted people to bow down and worship him, but Daniel wouldn't. Three times a day, Daniel knelt and prayed to God.

So the king made a rule that people must pray to him or be put in the den with hungry lions. Daniel knew he should only pray to God, no matter what the king said. So, sure enough, he ended up with the lions.

But—surprise!—God sent an angel to shut the lions' mouths! The next morning, when the king came to look, he found that Daniel didn't even have a scratch!

Dear God, Help me to be proud of You like Daniel. I want everyone to know I love You.

You and I never need to be embarrassed about praying to God, no matter what. We must remember that all the angels of heaven are on the side of those who love and obey God.

(Daniel 6)

16

Illustration by Tim Jonke

■　　■　　■

We live in a world where both good and bad things happen. Every day we hear news about wrong things people do. Another story about Daniel will help you understand why this is true.

Daniel felt very sad about all the bad things he saw happening. He talked to God and told Him how sorry he was for the wicked things people were doing.

Later, an angel named Gabriel flew swiftly to him.

"Do not be afraid, Daniel," said Gabriel. "I would have come even faster, but for twenty-one days I had to fight the prince of Persia. Another angel, Michael, helped me win the battle."

Dear God,
You love me so much
You have angels who can
keep me from evil.
Help me always
to remember that.

Imagine! God has strong warrior angels in the heavens, fighting against the evil angels of Satan's kingdom—guarding you from the evil one.

What do you think you would see if the sky were folded back? More angels than you could count, helping to protect you!

(Daniel 9 and 10)

18

Illustration by Scott Holladay

■　　　■　　　■

"You . . . have received the law that was put into effect through angels." Acts 7:53
". . . He came with myriads of holy ones from the south, from his mountain slopes." Deuteronomy 33:2

Do you have rules at your house? Your mom may say, "Don't talk with your mouth full" or, "You must tell the truth."

Many years ago God gave some rules that are still important today. We call these rules "the Ten Commandments." They tell us to worship only God, not idols, and never to steal or tell lies.

When God gave the Ten Commandments, thousands of angelic horsemen and royal chariot drivers watched. Maybe an angel trumpet player announced the laws with a fanfare. *Dah! Ta-dah!*

God wants us to think about His laws. "They are not just words," He says, "they are your life!" No wonder God brought angels with Him to announce these important commands.

(Exodus 20:3-17)

Dear God,
Help me always
to obey Your laws—
laws so important
Your angels helped
to announce them.

Illustration by Krystyna Stasiak

■　　　■　　　■

**"[Jacob] had a dream in which he saw a stairway [or ladder] resting on the earth, with its top reaching to heaven, and the angels of God were ascending and descending on it."
Genesis 28:12**

Imagine the longest ladder you have ever seen. Maybe it was on a fire truck that had a driver in the front and back. The ladder in this story is even longer than that.

Jacob was away from home on a trip and was very tired. He had just gone to sleep and was dreaming. In his dream, he saw angels going up and down a long, long ladder that reached all the way from earth to heaven.

God was at the top of the ladder. He told Jacob, "I will protect you wherever you go."

When Jacob woke up, he knew God was showing His love to him.

God used His angels to help Jacob not to be afraid. When you put your head on your soft pillow at night, remember that God's angels are watching over you, too.

(Genesis 28:10-22)

*Dear God,
Instead of just talking to
Jacob from heaven, You
used a ladder and angels.
What a good idea!
I know You're
watching over me
when I sleep, too.*

Illustration by Gustave Dore

■   ■   ■

"See, I am sending an angel ahead of you to guard you along the way and to bring you to the place I have prepared."
Exodus 23:20

When you go on a trip with your family, you need a map. It shows you which roads to take and where to turn.

The people in this picture were going on a trip. A man named Moses was their leader. His job was to take them from Egypt to their new home—but he didn't have a map. Instead, God sent an angel to guide and protect them!

God told the people to listen to the angel. If they obeyed, they would be safe. And since angels never get tired, the people would be watched over night and day. With an angel to guide them, Moses and the people didn't need a map.

God still uses His angels today. Close your eyes and try to imagine all the places they might be.

(Exodus 23:20-33)

Dear God, I'm thankful Your angel helpers never sleep. I'm glad they're all around me.

Illustration by David Slonim

■   ■   ■

"But the angel said to her, 'Do not be afraid, Mary, you have found favor with God. You will be with child and give birth to a son, and you are to give him the name Jesus.' "
Luke 1:30, 31

God has thousands and thousands of angels to help Him. The angel Gabriel has a special job of delivering important messages.

The most important message Gabriel ever delivered was to a young woman named Mary. He told her she was going to have a baby—Jesus! God had chosen her to be the mother of His Son.

This was the best news that had ever come from heaven to earth! Jesus, God's Son, came to save us from our sins. The world would never be the same again.

"Do not be afraid," Gabriel said to Mary.

And when Jesus is your best friend, you do not need to be afraid, either.

Dear God,
I'm glad You sent
Gabriel to tell Mary
the good news
about Jesus.
Thank You that Jesus
helps me
when I am afraid.

(Luke 1:26-38)

Illustration by Ron DiCianni

"Suddenly a great company of the heavenly host appeared with the angel, praising God and saying, 'Glory to God in the highest, and on earth peace to men on whom his favor rests.' "
Luke 2:13, 14

Dear God
I wish I could have been there the night Jesus was born, and seen the sky full of Your singing angels!
I'm happy that Jesus came to earth, too. I want to sing praises like the angels!

When you were born, everyone was excited. Grandmas, grandpas, friends and neighbors all came to look at you—the new baby!

When Baby Jesus was born, He had lots of visitors, too . . . but none were His grandpa or grandma. Jesus' mother, Mary, was far from home when He was born.

The inn was full, and there was no hospital in Bethlehem. Jesus was born in a stable with sleeping cows and sheep. So Mary and Joseph were very surprised to hear from the shepherds that the heavens had been full of singing angels.

Yes, when God wanted a giant celebration for Jesus' birth, He called on His wonderful angel helpers. Baby Jesus, God's Son, had so many angels to praise Him that only the sky could hold them!

(Luke 2:1-20)

Illustration by Richard Williams

■   ■   ■

"I tell you, there is rejoicing in the presence of the angels of God over one sinner who repents." Luke 15:10

*W*hen Jesus was on earth, He told lots of stories to His friends.

One day while He and His helpers were eating dinner, Jesus said, "A woman who had ten silver coins lost one."

(That would be like having ten shiny dimes and losing one of them in your bedroom.)

"She took a light, swept the house and looked carefully until she found it. Then she called her friends and neighbors together and said, 'Rejoice with me, I have found my lost coin.' "

Dear God, Thank You for loving me so much. I'm glad Your angels have a big party when someone asks Jesus into their life.

Jesus told this story so you would understand how much He loves you. You are worth more to Him than all the money in the world.

When you ask Jesus into your life, the angels get so excited they have a celebration. See how happy the angels in this picture look? Have they had a party for you?

(Luke 15:8-10)

Illustration by Jeanne Arnold